WISDOM TREE

Contents

1. **Generosity**   3

   A generous person will prosper; whoever refreshes others will be refreshed.

2. **Happiness**   14

   Be happy not because everything is good but because you can see the good in everything

3. **Cooperation**   23

   When was ever honey made with one bee in a hive?

4. **Honesty**   36

   Honesty is the best policy

5. **Respect yourself and others**   45

   Give respect; then you will get some back

6. **Care for the planet**   55

   "Earth provides for everyone's need but not for everyone's greed."

The Good Citizen in Me   64

Generosity

What is generosity?
Generosity is the quality of being kind and generous. It is the habit of giving freely without expecting anything in return. When you give, you should give wholeheartedly. We have been taught to acknowledge and thank the people who show generosity towards us.

Let us learn a bit more about the value of generosity from a Russian folktale.

Long ago, in Russia, there was a Tsar, who was really concerned about the welfare of his people. He often disguised himself as a traveller and went to villages in various parts of the country. He would first find out what ailed the people and what gave them peace and happiness.

Once, while on such a journey through the country in disguise, the Tsar was caught in a wild storm. It started snowing and soon the entire countryside was covered in thick snow. The Tsar was cold, hungry and lost.

Just as he thought of giving up hope, he spotted a warm light at a distance. With great difficulty, he got to the source of the light. It came from a very small shack. He knocked at the door of the shack. A shabby man opened the door.

The man was surprised to find a stranger at his door in the terrible storm. He immediately invited the stranger in and shut the door of the shack, to block out the cold wind. He then led the stranger to the warmest part of the small hut. This place was right by the side of the small fire built in the hut to keep the family warm.

The Tsar was grateful for the man's hospitality and the warm fire. While warming himself up, he noticed that the man lived with his wife and several children in the shabby hut. The hut was hardly furnished and the family was very poorly dressed.

The owner of the shack began asking the stranger who had come to his home, "Who are you stranger? Where do you come from and where are you headed? It is a terrible storm that is raging outside. It is lucky that you chanced upon my home. You could have died in that storm."

Before the Tsar could answer any of the questions the man had asked him, the Tsar began coughing uncontrollably. He had caught the cold. The poor man's wife immediately said, "Oh dear! You have caught the cold. I will brew you some chicken soup. That will make you feel better."

And so she set about making chicken soup with the only chicken (and a very thin one at that) they had in their hut. Once the soup was ready, the wife served all of it to the guest. The Tsar asked the man, his wife and their children to share the soup. However, they all refused. They said, "You need the soup more than we do. You are very sick. It will make you better."

The Tsar had it all. He was very grateful to the family. He said, "I want to reciprocate your kindness. But I am afraid whatever I give you will not be even remotely close to your generosity. He had made a mental note of the number of fat drops in the soup. He gave the family that many gold coins and revealed who he was. The family was now so rich that they no longer had to worry about food and warmth ever.

Soon word spread about the Tsar's reward. One rich man, who lived a few villages away, got to know about this. He somehow spotted the Tsar while he was returning to his palace. He pretended not to know about the Tsar's true identity and invited the Tsar to warm himself by the fireside in his home. The Tsar accepted the man's invitation. The man then served the Tsar chicken soup. After drinking the soup, the Tsar revealed his identity and offered to repay the man for his hospitality. He spotted only one thick layer of fat in the chicken soup, for the man was rich and his chickens were all fat. The Tsar therefore gave only one gold coin and left the greedy man's home.

Comprehension questions

Answer the following questions to check your understanding of the story.

1. Why did the Tsar go out disguised as an ordinary man?
   _____
   _____
   _____

2. Why was the Tsar on the verge of giving up hope for his life?
   _____
   _____
   _____

3. How did the poor man and his family show kindness and generosity to the Tsar?
   _____
   _____
   _____

4. What qualities in the poor man endeared him to the Tsar?
   _____
   _____
   _____

5. What qualities do you think the Tsar possesses? Which was the one that helped him find out that the other man who offered him soup was greedy for money.
   _____
   _____
   _____

6. What have you learnt about the value of generosity through this story?
   _____
   _____
   _____

More about the Value

Let us now understand why we need to be generous. First comes the natural answer that what you have in excess should be shared with those who do not have anything. This is also called *philanthropy*. When you give out of generosity, you feel good about yourself. You also gain happiness when you see the other person is benefitting from your generosity.

Another way of looking at generosity is giving away things for your own good. Have you ever noticed that the more things you have, the more time and effort you shell out to take care of these things and the lesser mental peace you have in safeguarding them? So, be generous and give away what you really don't need or what you can afford to give away. Then your room becomes less cluttered and your life easier.

Generosity will also make you less self-centered. Rather than focusing on yourself and your needs alone, you will be able to think of other people and their needs.

When you give freely, don't you think people will love you? Though you may like this feeling of being loved and looked upon, remember that it is not true generosity when you give while expecting something in return, be it gratitude, name or any material object.

Generosity does not demand anything in return. Sometimes you are generous because you feel like it. At other times you are generous because you consider it a duty. At times you are generous to people you know well. make space here where the new sentence starts. At other times, you are generous to even strangers.

> You don't need a reason to help people.   - Charles Dickens

Let us read the following snippet from the life of Mahatma Gandhi to understand another facet of generosity.

During the fight for freedom, Indians, under the leadership of Gandhiji, decided to quit using foreign loom products. They took to spinning cotton yarn at home, and wear clothes made indigenously. Gandhiji was collecting funds for this purpose.

He was in Orissa (now Odisha) and was requesting people to contribute to the fund. Many people made contibutions. An old woman with a bent back and frayed clothes walked up to him slowly. She placed a copper coin at Bapu's feet and left. The in-charge of the fund asked Gandhiji for the coin. Bapu refused to give the coin. The in-charge, with a smile said, "I take care of cheques worth hundreds of rupees and you don't trust me with a small copper coin?"

To this Gandhiji replied, "This copper coin is worth more than several hundreds. When a man has lakhs, and he gives away a few hundreds, it is okay. But when a person has almost nothing and gives the only coin she owns, its worth increases enormously."

A VALUE FOR ME
A generous person will prosper; whoever refreshes others will be refreshed.

Read this inspiring poem by John Wesley to get a clue on how to be generous.

> "Do all the good you can,
> By all the means you can,
> In all the ways you can,
> In all the places you can,
> At all the times you can,
> To all the people you can,
> As long as ever you can."

Exercises

1. In the word grid below, find out some of the synonyms and antonyms of the concept of generosity.

A	R	H	Y	E	U	V	D	N	G
F	T	M	G	H	V	W	K	H	R
T	D	I	H	T	C	S	I	J	E
H	G	S	E	Y	H	V	N	W	E
O	P	E	N	H	A	N	D	E	D
U	T	R	S	T	R	Z	H	N	Y
G	Y	L	A	D	I	X	D	B	P
H	J	Y	W	X	T	C	R	D	U
T	K	T	U	S	A	F	T	S	O
L	N	C	L	I	B	E	R	A	L
E	V	Y	K	D	L	U	U	D	V
S	B	U	L	P	E	J	I	H	W
S	E	L	F	I	S	H	L	A	Q

2. **Case Study:**

   Nepal Earthquake: Indian companies pulling out all stops to aid rescue mission, offering men, money and materials

   As the Indian government undertakes its biggest overseas relief and rescue mission in quake-hit Nepal, India Inc has got into the act as well, acting as a force multiplier to official efforts and adding to the country's most expansive overseas humanitarian intervention to date.

   From large conglomerates to tiny startups, corporate India is pulling out all the stops to aid the rescue mission in Nepal, offering men, money and materials on a scale never done in the past. From blankets to drinking water to medicines to food to discounted air fares to simply cash, a steadily growing parade of companies is committing resources to help the stricken neighbour, where the number of deaths crossed 4,000.

When disaster struck Nepal in the form of a series of earthquakes, the strongest measuring 7.9 on the Richter scale, many countries extended their hand to help Nepal cope up with the calamity. India was one of the first countries to offer help. Indian conglomerates came forward in offering aid. Find out the various kinds of aid that were sent to the people in Nepal. List them to understand the wide range of help that can be offered during any crisis.

Name of the Company / Organization	Aid Offered

3. Generous people show some particular traits and qualities. Complete the crossword to know these traits and qualities.

1. _ R U _ T _
2. _ N E _ S
3. _ E A D _ _ S
   G
4. _ T _ M I S _ T
5. _ L T _ U _ S _ I C

a. Generous people are not selfish. They can be _____ with any task.

b. Generous people devote most of their time and energy to help others. They are _____.

c. Generous people have the ability to lead because they can think of not just themselves but also others. They make good _____.

d. They think that the world can become a better place and they work towards that end. They are not pessimists. They are _____.

e. Generous people give without expecting anything in return. They are _____.

4. Which of the following would you consider as acts of generosity? Tick your answers.

- Blood donation (Generosity/Responsibility)
- Arriving at school on time (Generosity/Duty)
- Believing in environmental conservation (Generosity/Responsibility)
- Organ donation (Generosity/Obligation)
- Casting a vote (Generosity/Duty)
- Going on a vacation (Generosity/Indulgence)
- Following rules (Generosity/Duty)
- Donating money to an NGO (Generosity/Hobby)
- Taking the stairs instead of the elevator (Generosity/Being health conscious)
- Buying candles made by the blind society in your city (Generosity/Duty)
- Sending packets of food to the flood victims (Generosity/Indulgence)
- Lending medical help to the poor (Generosity/Duty)

5. Who among the following are generous people? Tick the correct box.

a. Soham checks his larder once in three months to identify any canned or packed food that he doesn't use. He then donates these to the poor.

   Generous   Not Generous

b. Rishabh and Rita don't mind giving away their old toys and books to poor people.

   Generous   Not Generous

c. Koel loves the pen that her grandfather gave her. She notices that her older sister cannot find her pen. So Koel gives her pen to her sister. After all, her sister cannot write an exam without a pen.

    Generous   Not Generous

d. Frieda loves books. She spends almost all her pocket money on buying books. She doesn't hold on to them though. Once she reads a book, she lends it to her friends.

    Generous   Not Generous

e. Every birthday, Aslam donates part of his gift money to the orphanage in his city.

    Generous   Not Generous

Test yourself

1. On receiving a bar of chocolate, do you ever say to your brother, sister or friend, "I will break it into two; you choose the portion that you want"?

2. Do you share freely with your friends?

3. Do you ever wish your cousins weren't around so that you could have a room to yourself at your grandparent's house?

4. On seeing a donation box at the counter of a shop or restaurant, do you feel like putting in some money?

5. Do you feel uncomfortable while thinking of visiting an orphanage?

    If your answers to the 1st, 2nd, 4th and 5th sentences are in the affirmative, you are a generous child.

*If you are uncomfortable about orphanages, it is perhaps because you are sensitive to the other child who doesn't have what you have. It only makes you a better person if you are sensitive and generous.

Tips to Parents and Teachers

Be role model for your child. Children learn by observing others around them. Emphasize that food and other natural resources like paper and petroleum should not be wasted. When we take only what we need, and not what we greed for, we are leaving things for others' use as well.

Also, make sure that you teach your child to be generous whenever it is required. Simple acts of sharing a chocolate, carpooling or donating to the poor are acts of generosity that children should be easily taught.

Teach children to be sensitive to other people—their suffering, their plight, their hunger and their compulsions. Make them understand how some people resort to menial and manual work because of compulsions. Help them sympathize and yet respect others.

Do's and Don'ts

What can you do?

- Donate food to the poor and the homeless.
- Visit an old age home or an orphanage and help them in whatever way you can.
- Recollect things that you are thankful for. Say the same in a prayer.
- Help people around you.
- Invite friends over on a festival and make them a part of your celebrations.
- Call up grandparents just to say you love them.
- Thank others for any kindness shown to you.
- Have your family adopt an orphan and help that person with this task..

Things you shouldn't do:

- Never waste food. Remember there are millions in the world who are starving.
- Be minimalistic. This means take only what you need. Gandhiji once said, "The world has enough for everyone's need and not for everyone's greed."
- Never expect anything in return when you are generous.
- Always help when you can.

Happiness

What is happiness?

Happiness, also known as joy is a state of the mind. You feel pleasant and generally have a smile on your face when you are glad or happy. Happiness is extremely important for mental and physical wellbeing.

Read the following story to know how one can attain happiness.

Many men live their life in pursuit of happiness. However, they do not know how to find it or where to find it.

Once, an old merchant wished happiness for his son. When his son grew up, the merchant asked his son tomeet about a wise old man who lived across the desert near their hometown. "This man," he told his son, "can teach you the meaning of happiness and show you how to achieve it."

The young boy set out to meet the wise old man. He spent many days and nights crossing the desert. He then also had to scale a tall mountain to reach the castle where the old man lived.

The boy expected to see an old man meditating in peace and quiet. But he was quite surprised to find a lot of activity in the castle. There were many people coming and going, people talking to each other in every corner, some more people playing soothing music and still others partaking of exquisite food from a huge table.

Amongst all this hustle and bustle, sat the wise old man, whom the boy had come to meet. Many were already waiting to talk to him. The young boy waited patiently for hours before he could get his turn to seek the advice of the old man.

After listening to the boy, the old man said, "I will explain to you the secret of happiness, but take a walk around the castle and come back a couple of hours later. We can talk then. While walking around the castle, I want you to carry a teaspoon filled with oil in it. Take care not to spill the oil."

The boy found the wise man's instructions quite strange. Yet he went around the castle with the spoon full of oil. As instructed, he returned a couple of hours later, pleased with himself because not a drop of oil had been spilt. The old man asked him, "Did you see the Persian tapestries in my dining room? Did you see the beautiful garden that the gardeners took a decade to create? Did you also see the rare books in my library?"

The boy was in a slight fix. He confessed that he hadn't noticed even a thing that the old man mentioned. "Now go back my boy, and see the wonders of my house."

The boy went once more to take a stroll around the castle. He returned after having marveled at the garden, the tapestries, the books and many other treasures. On his return, he praised the old man for all his treasures.

"I am glad that you are able to appreciate them. Now where are the two drops of oil?"

The boy realized that he had spilled the oil while marveling the castle.

The old man then said, "You have witnessed the secret to happiness my boy. Remember to look at the wonders of the world and yet never forget the two drops of oil in the spoon you hold."

From "The Alchemist" by Paul Coelho

Comprehension questions

Answer the following questions to check your understanding of the story.

1. What did merchant wish for his son?
   _____
   _____
   _____

2. Where did the merchant send his son across the desert and why?
   _____
   _____
   _____

3. What strange instructions did the old man give?
   _____
   _____
   _____

4. What happened to the oil in the spoon the second time the boy went around the castle? Why did this happen?
   _____
   _____
   _____

5. What according to the old man is the secret to happiness?
   _____
   _____
   _____

6. What do you think the oil in the spoon represents?
   _____
   _____
   _____

More about the Value

Happiness is the opposite of sadness. Nobody likes to be sad. Everyone wants to be happy. When you are happy, you feel on top of the world. You feel energetic. You feel good about yourself and also about others around you.

How to achieve happiness is something that you have to find out for yourself. For some, happiness comes from listening to music, singing or playing instruments, dancing, reading books, playing with friends, helping others and so on. What brings you happiness? Find out for yourself and list them out if you can.

People who are happy are known to be healthier too. So, it is for our wellbeing that we have to learn to be happy and not worry or become sad over many things in life. They say, 'When you cry, you cry alone, but when you smile, the whole world smiles with you.'

Therefore, be happy and make others happy.

> "Happiness is not something readymade. It comes from your own actions."
> — Dalai Lama XIV

> "For every minute you are angry you lose sixty seconds of happiness."
> — Ralph Waldo Emerson

A VALUE FOR ME

Be happy not because everything is good but because you can see the good in everything.

Snippet

Mullah Naseeruddin, while walking through the town came upon a man carrying a sack on his back. This man was looking very sad.

Unable to hold back, Naseeruddin asked the man, "Why are you sad, dear man?"

The man replied, "Do you see this sack on my back? All that I own is in this sack. This is all that I own in the world. How can I be happy with such a miserable and poor life?"

On hearing this, Naseeruddin did something unexpected. With great agility, he pulled the sack off the man's back and ran away with it.

"Wait! What are you doing? Come back with my sack, you thief. Help! Thief!" shouted the man while running behind Naseeruddin.

Naseeruddin was quite a fast runner. He rounded a corner, dropped the sack there and hid behind a tree."

In a short while, the man came running up the road and on seeing the sack stopped to pick it up. He checked its contents and smiled with relief.

Naseeruddin then came out from behind the tree and said, "You look happy to see your sack."

"Why wouldn't I be?" said the man, clinging onto his sack lest Naseeruddin would run away with it once again.

"That then teaches you to be happy with what you have and not fret for things that you don't have," said Naseeruddin and walked away leaving a perplexed man with the sack.

Exercises

1. **Look at the pictures below. Why do you think they are happy. Imagine the reasons and write them down.**

2. **Make a collage of things that make you happy.**

3. **Which of the following are true? Tick the correct box.**

    a. Happy children are healthier. True / False

    b. Happy children are a menace to others. True / False

    c. Happy children are more confident. True / False

    d. Happy children spread happiness amongst others. True / False

    e. Happy children can never be serious. True / False

    f. Happy children are more successful in life. True / False

    g. Happy children are easy to like. True / False

    h. You would want a happy friend rather than an unhappy one. True / False

4. **The following will help you attain happiness. Make these a habit. Begin by doing at least one thing from each of the following categories every day. Keep a record of the same for one week.**

Value / Activity	Monday	Tuesday	Wednesday	Thursday	Friday	Saturday	Sunday
Gratitude (Be grateful) What were you grateful for today?							
Kindness (Be kind) What was your act of kindness today?							

Indulge in a creative activity. (What creative activity you did today?)							
Exercise (What games have you played today? / How long have you exercised today?)							

Happiness is not something that comes to us overnight. We can be happy by training ourselves.

5. **Have you heard of a laughter club? Find out what laughter clubs do and what the benefits of a laughter club are. Prepare a pamphlet stating the advantages of laughter and happiness in life.**

   *A pamphlet is a small booklet or leaflet containing information about a topic.

Test yourself

Are you a happy person? Answer the following questions and check for yourself. Be truthful while answering the questions.

1. How are you feeling right now?

    a. Great ☐   b. Okay ☐   c. Bad ☐

2. Do you like helping others? Yes / No
3. When you get angry, do you believe in giving back? Yes / No
4. When you meet a person for the first time in the day, do you greet him or her? Yes / No
5. Do you like meeting people? Yes / No

*Question 1 will right away give you whether you are happy right now or not.

If your answers to the questions 2, 4 and 5 are in the assertive, you are a happy person. Else, you could start by following the points given in the Dos and Don'ts section to make yourself a happier person. Keep smiling, always.

Tips to Parents and Teachers

Happy parents and teachers make children happy. Therefore, invest time in making yourself happy. This in turn helps you enable the children to be happy.

Dos and Don'ts

1. A happy mind makes a healthy body. In turn, a healthy body also helps to keep you happy. Therefore, exercise daily.
2. Never let anger get the better of you. Whenever you are angry with yourself, someone or a situation, try to remain calm. Count (in your mind) to ten before you act. Never act in haste to repent later.
3. Keep smiling. It takes you lesser energy to smile than to frown. It makes you look like a friendly person. It also becomes a habit with time.
4. Never use bad language. Also, try not to talk negative about people.
5. Remember to eat healthy food and take ample rest.
6. Avoid sleeping late.
7. Be grateful to God for what you have.
8. Avoid jealousy.
9. Spend time with family. Relationships with friends and family will make you and them happy.

Cooperation

Meaning

Cooperation is helping each other. It is the process of working together to achieve a common goal. It is having tolerance for another person's viewpoint, respecting it and working alongside him or her. Cooperation is a very useful thing. You not only help each other, but you can also achieve better results through cooperation. It brings about happiness and lets you make friends.

Let us read a Norwegian folk tale to know a bit about cooperation.

In Norway, the kids are told of the story of a ram and its companions. Every day the ram was stuffed with food until it could take no more. It thought its farmer was kind and loving for giving it so much food. The ram was happy with its life on the farm.

And then one day, the farmer's wife came along. While giving the ram its daily food, the farmer's wife said, "Eat up little animal. You have very few days left. Soon we will have you on our dining table. You have fattened up well!"

On hearing this, the ram panicked. He tried getting out of the farm as soon as he could. He first went to the pig, his friend on the farm.

"Did you know why they feed us so much?" the ram asked the pig.

"Perhaps, because we are loveable and cute," answered the pig.

"No," replied the ram, "because they want to eat us when we are fat enough."

On hearing this, the pig too panicked. It also wanted to escape the farm.

"I plan to build a house for myself in the forest. If you want to you can come with me. But how will you help?" the ram asked the pig.

"I can push heavy logs," said the pig. The ram then said, "That's good. You can come with me then."

Soon, the two of them set out of the farm.

On their way out, they met a goose. "Where are you two headed on this fine day?" asked the goose.

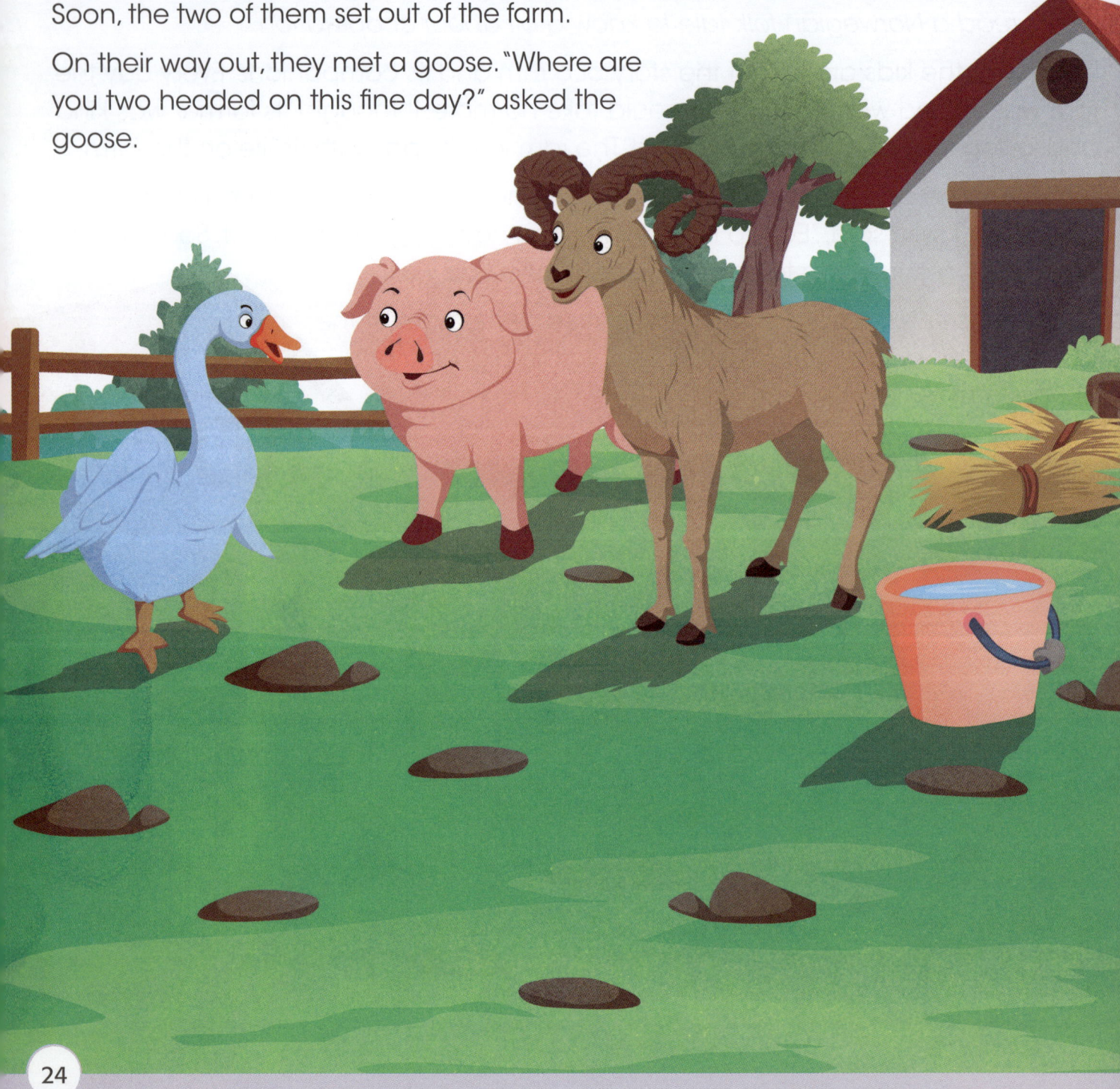

The ram and the pig told the goose why they were leaving the farm. The goose too panicked.

"Please, let me come with you. I have no intention of becoming a stuffed goose on their dining table," it cried.

"Oh, but what can you do? How can you help us?" asked the pig.

"I may be small and weak, but I am good at plucking. I can pluck moss and stick it into the gaps in the planks of the house that you plan to build," it said.

The ram and the pig agreed. Soon they ran out of the farm together with the goose.

Just as they neared the forest, they met a hare. "Three friends out on a stroll in the forest, is it?" said the hare.

"Oh no!" said the ram. "We found out why the farmer and his wife fed us daily. They want fat for a delicious meal on their table. So, we are now running away to the forest. We are going to build ourselves a fine house to live in."

The hare then said, "A house is it? I live in the bushes. But every winter, I keep thinking of having a warm cozy home to escape the cold. May I join you three? Can I stay with you in your house?"

"Yes, you may, but each one of us is helping with our special talents to build that house. How can you help build the house?" asked the goose.

"I have strong teeth. I can gnaw at the wood and work as a carpenter," said the hare.

The ram, the pig and the goose agreed to having the hare join them. They all went deeper into the forest.

Somewhere in the forest, they met a rooster. "What a curious band of friends," thought the rooster. "What are you doing here, animals of the farm? Have you lost your way," it asked them.

They explained why they had left their previous homes. They also told the rooster of their plan to build a house for themselves.

"I would also love to have a house to sit on. Can I join you all?" it asked.

"But how are you going to help us build the house?" asked the hare.

"I will be your clock," said the rooster. I will crow at the crack of dawn to wake you up. The rest of the animals liked the idea of having an alarm clock in their home. So they agreed to have the rooster also join their team.

When the five of them identified the place where they wanted their home to be, they set to work. The ram felled trees and the pig pushed them to the site. The hare worked as the carpenter and the goose stuffed moss and leaves into empty spaces between the logs. The rooster crowed diligently every morning, ensuring that the animals did not oversleep.

Soon the house was ready and the animals moved in.

Not far away from there, lived two wolves. They wanted to find out who their new neighbours were. One of the wolves went over. As soon as it entered the house, the ram butted him towards the stove. The wolf fell. Its head stuck in a pot. The pig then bit him hard. The goose began to peck him and the rooster crowed, creating an enormous racket. The hare ran all over the place.

The wolf with great difficulty managed to run out of the house, with its head still stuck in the pot.

When the other wolf got the pot off its mate's head, the first wolf said, "Strange creatures live in that house. They are very strong. They pushed me into the fire. They pinched me with tongs. I heard one of them running around looking for something,

perhaps a knife or a gun to kill me with. They also screeched in a scary voice from the roof. It is lucky that I got out alive."

The two wolves were now so scared for their lives that they decided to leave their home and head to another forest.

Once they left, the ram, the pig, the goose, the hare and the rooster were absolutely safe. They lived the rest of their lives in their home, in peace.

Comprehension questions

Answer the following questions to check your understanding of the story.

1. Why was the ram initially very happy with its life on the farm?
   _____
   _____

2. Why then did it decide to leave the comfort of the farm?
   _____
   _____
   _____

3. Which two animals from the farm wanted to go along with the ram? How did they each offer to help build the home?
   _____
   _____
   _____

4. How did the hare and the rooster offer to help build the home?
   _____
   _____
   _____

5. Why do you think each animal was asked how it could help build the home? Why were they not allowed to join in without volunteering to help?
   _____
   _____
   _____

6. Towards the end of the story, how did the animals benefit by sticking together?
   _____
   _____
   _____

More about the Value

Cooperation is working together. It is working together for a common goal. It is not necessary that everyone work on the same thing while cooperating. One may be doing a task, and the other, who is in no way connected to the task could still cooperate, and help the person. For example, in a pickling factory, once the pickles are ready, they are put into bottles and sealed off with a cap. These bottles and caps are made in another factory. Unless the bottles are made to specification, there is always the danger of the pickles getting spoilt or being rejected by the quality check department of a supermarket. In such a scenario, both the pickle factory and the bottle factory will suffer. Therefore, it is in their mutual interest that they work together, keeping each other's specifications, limitations and demands in mind.

Therefore, we can conclude that cooperation not only makes a task easier, but it also ensures that we do not waste resources while finishing the task. Cooperation leads to happiness, friendliness, sharing and progress.

In our county, we often hear of water disputes between states. If the states come to an understanding on how to share the water of the rivers, and cooperate with each other, we could use river water more efficiently and people in all the concerned states will benefit from this cooperation.

> In union there is strength.
>
> — Aesop

A VALUE FOR ME

When was ever honey made with one bee in a hive?

Snippet

When Prince Rama of Ayodhya had to save his wife Sita from the clutches of Ravana, an army of monkeys, the Vaanar Sena, helped him. They were told to throw the stones on the beach into the sea. These stones could float on water, and so a bridge could be built across the ocean to the island kingdom of Lanka. That was where Ravana held Sita captive.

While the large army of the monkeys were busy carrying stones and flinging them into the ocean, Rama observed a squirrel scurrying from beach to the bridge and back again. Curious, Rama approached the squirrel and saw that it was carrying small amounts of sand in its tiny hands. It poured the sand in between the rocks on the bridge. It was trying to fill the tiny gaps in the bridge.

Image of a squirrel pouring sand onto the bridge of stones being built by the Vaanar Sena, across the sea.

The squirrel was doing all it could to help build the bridge for Rama to cross over and defeat Ravana.

Co-operation is the sap of life,

Without which nothing can be realized;

Nor harmony be really devised

Amidst children/ citizens/husband/ wife.

No department can flourish without it;

No army however strong wins the war;

No earthly telescopes can reach a star,

Sans co-operation, a good habit.

Co-operation brings success in life,

In one's family or in his work-spot;

And decides progress or a nation's lot,

Solving, modifying, postponing strife.

One can succeed if spouse co-operates;

Man succeeds whenever God operates!

Dr John Celes

Exercises

1. Cooperation is not merely between two people. It is also between countries. Find out at least one country with which India has cooperative ties. Write how the two countries benefit by cooperating with each other.

   _____
   _____
   _____
   _____
   _____
   _____
   _____
   _____

2. Using the words below, create a story to convey that cooperating is essential.

   | A thirsty lion | a thirsty boar | a pond of water | a fight | vultures waiting to peck on the dead animal |

   _____
   _____
   _____
   _____
   _____
   _____
   _____
   _____
   _____
   _____
   _____
   _____

3. Let us learn from some well-known stories and incidents. Identify which of the following characters are cooperative. Put a tick or a cross accordingly in the boxes.

   a. Harry Potter gets to know that all the contestants have to fight a dragon each. He lets this secret out to the competitors. He wants a fair play.

   ☐

   b. The lion lets go the mouse without killing it. The mouse later saves the lion from the hunter's net. Is this an example of cooperation?

   ☐

   c. Rama helps Sugreeva to kill Vaali, in return for the help of the Vainer army. Is this an example of cooperation?

   ☐

   d. The crocodile loves his wife so much that he agrees to bring her his friend the monkey's heart. The monkey too agrees to give his heart, but only as a means to escape from the clutches of the crocodile.

   ☐

4. Put on your thinking caps and answer the following:

   a. Have you ever refused to cooperate with a friend or a family member? If so, why?

   _____
   _____
   _____

   b. How do you feel when someone refuses to cooperate with you?

   _____
   _____
   _____

   c. If a person in your classroom refuses to be cooperative, how would you make him or her cooperate?

   _____
   _____
   _____

d. What rules would you put into place to encourage all children in your class and all the people in your home cooperate?

_____

_____

_____

5. Create your own jingle or arap to convey the merits and need for cooperation in our country today.

_____

_____

_____

_____

_____

_____

_____

_____

_____

_____

_____

_____

_____

_____

_____

Test yourself

Are you a cooperative person? Check for yourself by answering the following questions.

1. Do you hate participating in teams? ☐
2. Are you willing to share your ideas with others? ☐
3. Do you listen attentively to others when they speak? ☐
4. If there is a task that nobody wants to do, do you back out? ☐
5. When there is a task that nobody wants to do, do you suggest that everyone needs to take turns in doing the task? ☐
6. When you are involved in an argument, do you always want to win the argument? ☐
7. When you are involved in an argument, do you sometimes compromise? ☐
8. Do you do a task to the best of your ability, even though there is nobody to notice it? ☐

If your answers to questions 1, 4 and 6 are in the assertive, then you need to work on building a cooperative attitude. If the rest of your answers are positive, continue the good work. Remember that cooperation leads to success and wellbeing of all.

Tips to Parents and Teachers

Cooperation is not merely the willingness to work in teams or to help others. It is also the ability to live in such a way so as not to cause inconvenience to others. It is also the willingness to live in such a way so as not to hurt the emotions, sentiments and beliefs of others.

Ensure that children to greet neighbours and friends whenever they meet. Encourage children to help an elderly person in the lift (volunteer to unlock their home for them, or carry their shopping bag for them to their door, etc.). Supervise the upkeep of common areas around your home. Always dump garbage only in the dustbin. Never party with loud music when a neighbour is ill or has examinations. Inform people living above or below your flat if there is any repair work happening at your place, so that they may protect themselves from the dust and sound.

Remember, cooperation starts from home.

Dos and Don'ts

Always	Never
1. Include everyone in your team. 2. Do the very best you can. 3. Agree to compromise if it is best for everyone involved. 4. Compliment or appreciate when someone does a good job or helps you. 5. Share you things, thoughts and ideas with others. 6. Listen when the other person speaks.	1. Isolate anyone even if they are not adept at doing it as well as the other person in the team. 2. Prolong an argument. 3. Ridicule the work done by anyone. 4. Refuse help from someone when he or she volunteers. It is both rude and suggestive that you don't like cooperation. 5. Leave your bit of work to be done by another person.

Honesty

Meaning
Simply put, honesty is speaking the truth. It also means being truthful to yourself and others. If you are fair and truthful, do not lie or cheat and above all live by good values, you are an honest person. Honesty is a value that helps you live in peace with yourself, and also wins the trust and hearts of others because you are then a dependable person. Honesty comes with self-discipline.

Rebecca's Afterthought

Yesterday, Rebecca Mason,

In the parlor by herself,

Broke a handsome china basin,

Placed upon the mantel-shelf.

Quite alarmed, she thought of going

Very quietly away,

Not a single person knowing,

Of her being there that day.

But Rebecca recollected

She was taught deceit to shun;

And the moment she reflected,

Told her mother what was done;

Who commended her behavior,

Loved her better, and forgave her.

— Elizabeth Turner

Whatever Brawls Disturb the Street

Once there was a little boy,
With curly hair and pleasant eye—
A boy who always told the truth,
And never, never told a lie.
And when he trotted off to school,
The children all about would cry,
"There goes the curly-headed boy—
The boy that never tells a lie."

And everybody loved him so,
Because he always told the truth,
That every day, as he grew up,
'Twas said, "There goes the honest youth."
And when the people that stood near
Would turn to ask the reason why,
The answer would be always this:
"Because he never tells a lie."

— Isaac Watts

Comprehension questions

Answer the following questions to check your understanding of the story.

1. What did Rebecca Mason drop?
   _____
   _____
   _____

2. 'Not a single person knowing that she was there that day.' How did this matter to Rebecca Mason?
   _____
   _____
   _____

3. How did owning up her mistake make Rebecca an honest person?
   _____
   _____
   _____

4. Why was the curly haired boy very popular?
   a. Because he had pleasant blue eyes
   b. Because he never told a lie.

5. When the curly haired boy grew up, why did everyone call him an honest person?
   _____
   _____
   _____

6. Both Rebecca and the curly haired boy did not lie and were hence honest. Can you tell one additional detail that Elizabeth Turner talks of in her poem.
   _____
   _____
   _____

More about the Value

We have read earlier that honesty is not lying. Telling the truth alone does not make you an honest person. Honesty is also about the ability to live the truth. Sometimes, it is easier to lie. For instance, you lie so that you do not hurt your friend or a younger sibling. Sometimes you lie to make your parents happy. But this is not honesty.

> Honesty is more than not lying. It is truth telling, truth speaking, truth living, and truth loving.
> James E. Faust

Honesty requires courage. It requires the strength to be able to tell the truth at all times, even though you may hurt others or may be hurt yourself. Though your friends or your family may be upset with you for telling the truth, with time, your truth is what will save you and them and help everyone lead a better life. For instance, you may lie to a friend that he or she is the best singer in the class, even though that person is not. Had you told the person the truth, you would have perhaps encouraged him or her to work harder at becoming better at the art. You would have saved them the grief of not being awarded the best singer award.

> It takes courage and strength to admit the truth. However, it is better than lies and deceit.

A VALUE FOR ME

With self-discipline, almost anything is possible.

Snippet

This is a true story of Peter, a newspaper vendor, who lives in Kerala. Along with newspapers, he also sells lottery tickets in his stall. Murugan, a humble man, who earns a living by pressing clothes, visits Peter's stall regularly. Murugan is in the habit of purchasing lottery tickets, hoping that lady luck would visit him someday.

Murugan always selected his lottery tickets and requested his friend Peter to put them aside for him. He would then go on to work and in the evening, while returning home, would pay for the lottery tickets with the money in his pocket. This was a habit with him.

Just like every other day where he visited Peter's stall, on the fateful day where our story took place, Murugan identified his lottery ticket. Having no money to pay immediately for it, he told Peter to put it aside for him, so that he could collect it in the evening. He then went on to press clothes.

Later that day, Peter got to know that the ticket that Murugan had selected had won Rs 40 Lakhs and a car. Technically, Murugan had no right on that ticket since he had not yet paid for it. However, honest Peter immediately informed Murugan to come and collect his ticket and then claim the money and car.

Peter did not put himself in the way of temptation and claim the prize money and gift for himself. He could have very easily done so and no one would have known of it. However, honest that he was, he saw to it that Murugan got his prize.

Exercises

1. **Complete the following sentences which are about honesty. Choose your answers from the words in the box.**

   | Lie | Honesty | Against | You | Right | Truths | Anyone |
   | Whole | True | Book | Policy | | | |

   a. Honesty is the best _____.

   b. Tell a _____ and all your _____ become questionable.

   c. Being honest never hurts _____. Being a liar hurts only _____.

   d. No legacy is as rich as _____.

   e. Being honest may not always get you many friends, but it will always get you the _____ ones.

   f. If it is not right, do not do it. If it is not _____, do not say it.

   g. Honesty is the first chapter in the _____ of wisdom.

   h. Who lies for you will also lie _____ you.

   i. A half-truth is a _____ lie.

2. **Find seven antonyms for honesty in the following word grid. To help you along, you can find words beginning with C, L, D, E, F, D and C.**

```
C A R E F U L O P L A
R C B D E C E I T Y L
I S T I Q W E E V I L
B D S S D W G H F N O
B S C H E A T I N G E
I C K O C M Z D C V R
N A W N V F S E F D D
G C Q E Y B N J S J H
F A L S E H O O D I M
A S K T E E R F U L C
C V R Y W E T Y S F S
C O R R U P T I O N R
```

3. Answer the following honestly.

a. Are you an honest person? Write any two reasons why you think so.

_____
_____
_____

b. How do you feel when someone is dishonest with you.

_____
_____
_____

c. If someone is dishonest with you, how would you deal with it?

_____
_____
_____

d. How can you make others be honest with you?

_____
_____
_____

4. **What will you do?**

Your parents give you an expensive watch for your birthday. You know they worked hard and saved up to give you this gift. But you don't really like it. What will you do? Will you tell them you didn't like it? Will you take it, thank them and wear it? Express and explain your actions in 50 to 100 words. Also, discuss if it is okay to lie under such circumstances.

5. Read the story of Pinocchio. Explain in your own words the value of honesty in context of this story.

_____
_____
_____
_____
_____
_____
_____
_____
_____
_____

6. Do you feel all advertisements on television or in the newspaper are honest? Identify one such advertisement that you find is completely honest or dishonest. State the advertisement. If you think it is honest, support yourself with proof or justification. If you think it is dishonest, then how would you change the advertisement to make it honest.

Be as creative as you can. Prepare your findings and justifications as a pamphlet.

Test yourself

1. You say that you always speak the truth, but you know that you don't.
2. You don't mind speaking good and bad about your friends. But you do it only when they are not around and with others.
3. Your mother is very particular that you eat all the food that she packs for you. Since you don't like what she gives you but prefer what your friend gets and since he likes what you get, you both exchange food daily and conveniently don't tell your mother so. You feel okay about it.
4. You find a thousand rupee note on the road. You don't know whom it belongs to. You feel uneasy keeping it for yourself or spending it on yourself.
5. You are playing chess. Your opponent gets up to attend to the phone call she received. You very cleverly move a pawn or two to help you win the game.

   *If you have said 'yes' to scenarios 1 and 4, you are an honest person. Good work! Keep it up!

   If you have answered the others with a 'no', even then you are an honest person. Remember, it takes courage and strength to own up to your faults and be honest. However, you need to work on being an honest person.

Tips to Parents and Teachers

Model honesty to the children not merely through words but also through actions. Many believe that white lies are essential for getting along in our world. However, the distinction between white lies and lies that can harm others is very slight, and it is easy to cross the border without knowing it. Therefore, insist on honesty at all times. Instill self-confidence and self-esteem in children. A confident child will not find the need to be dishonest.

Do's and Don'ts

1. Speak the truth always. Remember that a lie comes round always.
2. Try not to lie, even if you feel it is necessary.
3. The truth you speak may affect or hurt someone. Speak thoughtfully and politely.
4. Keep your promises. Make promises that you can keep. Never make promises that you cannot keep.
5. Honesty reflects in your speech and actions. Ensure that you practice what you preach.
6. Be on time, complete assignments in time.
7. Never cheat or copy. If you have borrowed ideas or content from someone or somewhere, acknowledge.
8. Thank all those that help you.

Respect Yourself and Others

> **Meaning**
> Respect is recognizing the dignity of a person or thing and honouring it. We could be respecting others or ourselves. We could be respecting people or their ideas, countries and culture. Respecting others means not hurting them; and taking into consideration their feelings, ideas and thoughts.
>
> Forcing our ideas and beliefs onto others is not respect. Belittling our culture of beliefs to ensure that others are not hurt is also not respect. Respect is maintaining your own beliefs and dignity and at the same time, living in a way that does not harm the dignity of others

Let us read a story from the Panchatantra that elucidates the value of respect.

In the city of Vardhamana, somewhere in ancient India, there lived a very clever merchant. Such was his capability to solve issues and give suggestions, that he was one of the most trusted aides of the King. Because of his closeness to the King, the merchant enjoyed immense respect within the kingdom. He had easy access to the royal palace too. He could come and go as he wished with no one to stop him or run a security check on him.

The merchant's daughter was getting married. He arranged for a large and lavish ceremony. Every important person in the kingdom, right from the King and his family to all serving officials at the palace were invited. Fellow merchants were also invited. So were the city's common folk like the vegetable vendors, the washer men and the sweepers. In short, almost every man, woman and child in the city was invited for the wedding at the merchant's home.

Everyone was having a good time at the wedding. So much fun did one particular person, who worked as a sweeper in the royal chambers, have, that he forgot protocol. He went and sat in the tent that was reserved for the royalty and the nobles.

The merchant happened to be passing by and noticed the palace sweeper seated on one of the fine chairs kept aside for the ministers. He got enraged and had the sweeper thrown out of the wedding.

The sweeper felt humiliated. Unable to forget the insult meted out to him, he decided to take revenge on the merchant. One morning, he was sweeping the king's sleeping chambers. The king was still on his bed. He was just waking up. The sweeper saw this and mumbled, "How ill-mannered the merchant has become. How could he embrace the queen?"

On hearing this, the king, now almost fully awake, got enraged. "How dare you say such a thing? Have you really seen the merchant embrace the queen?" he asked the sweeper.

"Forgive me, my lord. I was busy the whole night. I hardly slept. I don't know what I said just now," said the sweeper.

The king let the sweeper go. But the seed of doubt and mistrust had been sowed in his mind. Soon, the king's treatment of the merchant changed. He was no longer friendly with the merchant. One day, as the merchant was entering the palace to meet the king, the guards stopped him. "You can no longer enter the palace

without permission. Please wait in line with the rest of the people who wish to enter the palace to meet the king," they told him.

The merchant was taken aback. He did not know what had caused the sudden change in the king's treatment.

Just then, the sweeper was passing by. He mumbled once again, as if speaking to the guards, "Let him go inside. You don't know how close he is to the king. He will have you insulted just the way he insulted me at his daughter's wedding. He will have you thrown out of your jobs."

On hearing this, the merchant realized what had caused all this change. He apologized to the sweeper and said, "I am sorry. I ought not to have insulted you at the wedding. Please come to my house." So he took the sweeper home, fed him a sumptuous lunch, and gave him lavish gifts. He promised to respect one and all, irrespective of who they were from that onwards.

The sweeper, now satisfied with the merchant's apology, decided to set things right between the king and the merchant. The next morning, while he was sweeping the king's sleeping quarters, he once again waited for the king to wake up.

He then mumbled, "How crazy is our king. Why does he eat his breakfast in the lavatory?" On hearing this, the king was once again enraged. "Where have you heard that I eat my breakfast in the lavatory? Who dare spread such humiliating rumours?"

The sweeper was once again ready with his excuse. He said, "Please dear king, I gambled through most of the night. I hardly slept. I do not know what I am talking of. I am barely awake now."

The king let the sweeper go after warning him never to gamble or sleep late again. He then thought, "Just as it is false that I eat my breakfast in the lavatory, it must be false that the merchant embraced the queen."

Comprehension questions

Answer the following questions to check your understanding of the story.

1. Why was the merchant greatly respected in the kingdom?
   _____
   _____
   _____

2. Why did the merchant throw the sweeper out of the wedding?
   _____
   _____
   _____

3. Why did the sweeper mumble in the king's chambers?
   _____
   _____
   _____

4. What did the merchant realize when he overheard what the sweeper told the guards at the palace gates?

   _____
   _____
   _____

5. What do you understand about respecting others from this story?

   _____
   _____
   _____

More about the Value

Respect is about being open-minded. It is about being tolerant towards others, their beliefs and their lifestyles. Secularism is respecting other religions. Maintaining law and order is also respecting the safety and freedom of other fellow citizens. Following rules is also respecting the authority and welfare of other people.

Respect also means being grateful for what you have and being considerate towards others. One may not like another person, but that does not give us the right to be disrespectful to that person. By being well mannered, one is respecting others.

> "Respect for ourselves guides our morals; respect for others guides our manners"
> — Laurence Sterne

By being self-disciplined, one is respecting one-self. Self-respect is also very important. You should live your life in such a way that you should be happy with yourself and should also be able to respect yourself.

> "Respect yourself and others will respect you."
> — Confucius, Sayings of Confucius

Every person, no matter what his or her status in society is, deserves respect.

> "I speak to everyone in the same way, whether he is the garbage man or the president of the university."
> — Albert Einstein

When you respect everyone, you also realize that you can learn from others and benefit from their experience. We are asked to respect especially our elders because we have a lot to learn from their lifetime of learning, knowledge and wisdom.

A VALUE FOR ME
Give respect; then you will get some back.

Snippet

Our country was plagued by the concept of untouchability. People of certain castes were not considered worthy of respect because of their lowly status in the society and also because of their birth. There is a beautiful story from the stories of the Buddha that teaches us that respect is not given because of the status in society but because of a person's deeds.

There was once a small village somewhere in central India. In that village lived a person called Sunnita. He earned his living by sweeping roads. His income was hardly enough to support himself. He had no home and slept by the roads. The people of the village never mingled with him. They hardly spoke to him too because he was of a lowly birth. He was required to move away from the road whenever any other person from the village walked on it. Even his shadow was considered inauspicious and was ordered off the roads. Such was his miserable life.

One day, Buddha along with his followers, was travelling through this village. Sunnita wanted to have a glimpse of the great Buddha. But he was afraid to stand anywhere near the road because he was considered inauspicious. So he climbed onto a tree at a distance and watched Buddha from there. Much to his shock and surprise, Buddha got off the road and walked to the tree on which Sunnita sat. He looked up and said, "My dear man, I see goodness in you. You have always helped others in your village without expecting anything in return. Would you like to leave here and follow me? Would you like to become my disciple?"

The shocked Sunnita was elated. With folded hands, he followed the Buddha. He became a monk. From then on, no one considered Sunnita inauspicious. He was always respected as the follower of the Buddha. Even kings bowed down to him in respect.

Exercises

1. Which of the following qualities will help you win respect? Tick your answers and cross out the others.

    a. Politeness ☐   b. Cunning ☐

    c. Fairness ☐   d. Trustworthy ☐

    e. Abusive ☐   f. Reliability ☐

    g. Being two-faced ☐   h. Being a good listener ☐

    i. Being Dominating ☐   g. Disobeying laws ☐

2. Create your own mutual respect wheel. Let this serve as a guide for you to learn how to respect others and also have them respect you.

    Two have been done for you. Fill up the other slots with your own rules.

    ### My Mutual Respect Wheel

    Respect other people's belongings. Take care not to damage them.

    When there is a problem, voice yourself peacefully. Listen to the other person too.

3. Have you ever pondered why we are asked to respect national symbols, religious symbols, and so on? List a few symbols that you respect.

    _____
    _____
    _____
    _____

4. **Following are some guidelines on what to do and not to do with a national flag. Fill in the blanks to complete the sentences. Choose your answers from the words given in the box.**

| Avoid | Step | Clean | Toys | Torn | Height |

a. Hoist the flag at a _____ so that it is visible to people from a distance.

b. _____ buying plastic flags. They are not good for the environment.

c. Do not let children use national flags as _____.

d. Ensure that the national flag is always _____ and never _____.

e. Never _____ on a national flag.

5. **Read the following poem. Later, answer the questions that follow.**

When I born, I Black,

When I grow up, I Black,

When I go in Sun, I Black,

When I scared, I Black,

When I sick, I Black,

And when I die, I still black..

And you White fella,

When you born, you Pink,

When you grow up, you White,

When you go in Sun, you Red,

When you cold, you Blue,

When you scared, you Yellow,

When you sick, you Green,

And when you die, you Gray.

And you calling me Colored?

Think and Answer

1. Who do you think the poet is?
    a. A person who has played Holi ☐   b. A person who is of African origin ☐
2. What do you think the poem is about?
    a. Racism ☐   b. The different phases of life ☐
3. Does the poet like being called 'coloured'?
    a. Yes ☐   b. No ☐
4. Have you ever called people names? If so, do you think you were correct in doing so?
    _____
    _____
    _____

5. Why is it not correct to call people names?
    _____
    _____
    _____

Test yourself

1. Do you expect everyone to listen to you? _____
2. Do you need to be reminded to thank an uncle who has sent you a gift?_____
3. Do you cross the roads only at a zebra crossing?_____
4. When in a queue, do you let the elderly lady behind you go first through the counter? _____
5. Do you wish your neighbour whenever you meet him or her? _____

    *If the answers to questions 1 and 2 are 'yes', then you need to learn to respect others. Else, remember always that respect begets respect. If you respect others, others will eventually respect you.

> Do unto others, as you would have them do unto

Tips to Parents and Teachers

You cannot give in to children all the time. You have to establish some rules for the family, for the classroom, for the school and also for the home. By following these rules, children learn to respect authority and in turn become sensitive, caring and helpful towards others. By not insisting that children follow these rules, you as a parent or a teacher will be heralding the child towards a failed future.

Respect does not come out of fear. Respect comes out of being able to identify or know what is to be done, what is to be appreciated and what is expected. Therefore, teach children to know for themselves what is good and what is bad.

Do's and Don'ts

1. Thank people for their kindness, help, and any other such gesture.
2. Never wait for someone to prompt you on your manners. You are grown up enough to know your manners.
3. Don't tolerate rudeness. However, rudeness is not an answer to rudeness. If someone is being rude to you, you can point it out politely. Don't however be rude to that person.
4. You cannot demand respect. You can only command it. This means that you cannot force someone to respect you. They will respect you if your actions are good.
5. Respect the aged and the young; the rich and the poor. Everyone deserves to be respected.

Care for the Planet

Meaning
One of the most important values that we need to inculcate today is perhaps to care for our planet. Mother earth provides for the nourishment of all living creatures. If its health declines, it will no longer be able to provide for and nourish them. safeguarding the fragile ecosystem on earth, maintaining its balance, and ensuring that human activity does not contribute to the decline and degradation of the planet's health is nothing but taking care of the planet.

Here is a folktale that makes us think about what we owe to the planet.

Long ago, in a faraway country, where the days and nights are very cold, there lived a boy called Mikku. It was his duty to gather firewood to keep his home and family warm. Once, while out in the forest, he thought to himself, "Until now, for all the firewood I need, I have been gathering fallen branches from the forest floor. But since I have grown big and strong, maybe I should chop trees. It would be easier than bending down to gather twig after twig, branch after branch."

So, he looked around to spot the right tree to chop down. He spotted a good one. No sooner did he raise his axe to cut down the tree, he heard a voice.

"Stop! Please don't cut me down." The tree was talking to him. In those days, humans could understand the language of the trees. The tree continued, "I am a birch tree. People use my bark to make baskets and brooms. I am very useful. So don't cut me down."

Mikku agreed. Indeed, the birch tree was quite useful. It would be a waste to cut it down. So he looked around for another tree. On spotting an ideal one, he once again raised his axe and once again he heard the tree speak to him.

"Stop! Don't cut me down. I am very useful to you. I am a cherry tree. My cherries make your pies and cakes tasty."

That was indeed true. Mikku loved cherries. So he agreed not to cut down the cherry tree too. When he spotted another tree that would be good for firewood, he once again picked up his axe and once again, the tree spoke to him. "I am an apple tree. I give you apples to munch. Please don't strike me down."

Mikku once again agreed not to cut down the tree. However much he tried to chop down a tree, he couldn't. All the trees in the forest were useful in one way or another. They all had only one thing to tell him, "You care for us and we will care for you."

So finally, he decided to go back to gathering fallen branches to serve as his firewood. When he was about to go on his job, a strange dwarfish person appeared before him. He had leaves for clothes, acorns for a hat and bark for boots. He said, "I am the elf of the forest. Since you have been good to the trees, I will reward you."

He gave Mikku a wand. He said, "You have been good to Nature. Now Nature will help you. Whenever you need anything from Nature, just wave your wand. You will receive it. If you need your land ploughed, wave it at the moles. They will do it for you. If you need honey, wave the wand at the bees. They will get it for you. But remember, never use the wand to go against Nature."

Thrilled with his magical wand, Mikku returned home. He wanted to test it. He waved it at some bees and requested them for honey. Soon, the sweetest honey he had ever tasted was before him. Next, he wanted some fruits. The birds went about gathering fresh fruits and dropped them all in his fruit bowl."

The moles ploughed his fields, the birds sowed the seeds and the clouds watered them. Mikku soon became rich, but lazy too. He became so used to using his wand, that he very forgot the instructions given by the forest elf.

Mikku hated the cold season. One morning, on a cold day, Mikku ordered the sun to come out from behind the clouds and shine on him to make him warm.

But this was against Nature. How could a cold winter morning have a warm shining sun? The wand flew away from Mikku's hand and disappeared into the forest, never to be seen again.

Since then, we humans have lost the ability to understand the language of the trees. We can only hear them whisper to each other. But they say, if you listen carefully, you can faintly make out the words, "You care for us and we will care for you."

Comprehension questions

Answer the following questions to check your understanding of the story.

1. Why did the boy want to chop down trees with his axe?

   _____
   _____
   _____

2. Why did every tree plead with the boy not to cut them down?
   _____
   _____

3. Mikku agreed and gave in to every tree's plea. He did not strike them down. What can you tell of Mikku's character from this gesture?
   _____
   _____
   _____

4. Why did the elf of the forest gift Mikku? What was the gift?
   _____
   _____
   _____

5. The elf had spoken of a condition while giving the gift. What was that condition?
   _____
   _____
   _____

6. How did Mikku break his promise to the elf? What happened there on?
   _____
   _____
   _____

More about the Value

Our planet is so far the only known planet in the entire universe to have life on it. Innumerable factors like the right distance from the sun, the presence of water and an atmosphere, the right amount of oxygen in the atmosphere, and so on, have allowed for the evolution of life on it. Our planet has seen life in different forms over millions of years. It is only recently that human beings have started to tap the resources of the planet for their own gain. Usage is fine, but over usage and abuse is not.

Knowingly or unknowingly, we have created an irreversible damage to our fragile planet. Gaping holes in the ozone layer, air and water pollution, soil erosion and deforestation, extinction of species are only a few of these damages. If we continue thoughtlessly with our abuse of the planet, we may no longer have a planet to live on. Our species may no longer be alive!

Therefore, it is our responsibility to take care of our planet. This is not merely the responsibility of the heads of countries or huge organizations but the responsibility of each and every one of us. Even if you plant one tree and take care of it, you will be doing your bit to take care of the planet.

> Earth provides to satisfy everyone's needs but not everyone's greed."
> — Mahatma Gandhi

A VALUE FOR ME
"Earth provides for everyone's need but not for everyone's greed."

Snippet

> "If the bee disappeared off the face of the earth, man would only have four years left to live."
> — Maurice Maeterlinck, The Life of the Bee

Bittu Sahgal lives in Mumbai. Even as a child, he polished shoes, delivered packages and did other odd jobs. If you thought he did all this to earn a living because he was poor, you are wrong. Apart from doing odd jobs, he also demanded toll from all visitors to his home.

All this he did to raise money to save our national animal. Such was his dedication to this cause he believed so much in, that even before he was ten years old, he had collected about 1.65 lakh rupees. He donated all this money to a foundation to protect tigers.

Exercises

1. **Solve the crossword puzzle by filling in suitable words. If you supply an apt word, you will also be listing out ways in which you can care for the planet.**

   Across:
   1. _____ the usage of paper napkins and cups. Switch to cloth hankies and regular cups.
   2. _____ off any lights or fans when no one is in the room. Avoid using them when natural light and breeze are available.
   5. Brush your teeth without _____ water. Use a cup.
   7. Use newspapers to _____ your gift. It is the heart with which you give that is important, not the quality of paper in which you give it.
   8. Use _____ transport whenever possible.
   9. Cars and bikes should be regularly _____.

   Down:
   1. Use _____ batteries.
   3. _____ dry clothes instead of using the drier.
   4. Use e-_____ while travelling. You can save paper.
   6. _____ a plant on your friend's birthday.
   8. Encourage car _____.

2. **Write an article in 250 words on the impact of human activity on global temperature.**

   (Clues: Increased human industrial activity, dependence on machines, emission of greenhouse gases, changes in weather patterns)

3. What would you consume less and waste less in order to protect and save our environment.

Consume Less	Waste Less

4. Prepare a brochure explaining how your generation can save the planet. You should include the following in your brochure.

- Why is there a need to care for the planet
- What you could do to save the planet
- What our country should do to save the planet

5. Activity: Bring a sample of the various things you can recycle to your school. Display them to your classmates. Put a collection bin in your school. Once you have collected them, arrange for them to be taken to a recycling plant.

- Aluminum
- PET plastic bottles (bottles containing beverages)
- Papers and cardboard
- Metal cans
- HDPE Plastic bottles (shampoo bottles, oil bottles, etc.)
- Computers / CDs
- Glass bottles
- Plastic (Covers, bottle caps, etc.)
- Compact Fluorescent Bulbs

Test yourself

1. Do you want your parents to take you out on long drives in your car because you enjoy them?
2. Do you use
a. Aluminum foils in your school lunch box?
b. Disposable cups?
c. Polythene bags?
3. Do you carry a cloth bag to the market and refuse polythene carrybags?
4. Do you hate not having greenery around you?
5. Do you not like to use hand me down books?

   *If your answers to questions 3 and 4 are yes, then you are concerned about your planet.

Tips to Parents and Teachers

This world is not ours to use as we wish. It is a gift we have borrowed from our future generations. Just as with any borrowed thing, it is our duty to return it in a good and usable condition. Cut down as much as you can on using our non-replenishable natural resources. Our habits become our culture. If we develop nature friendly-habits, our collective culture will be planet friendly. This, in return, will help save our planet.

Do's and Don'ts

1. Say no to plastics.
2. Cut down on the usage of disposable plates, cups and tissues.
3. Inculcate the habit of using cloth handkerchief.
4. Live and let live. Let other living things, both from the plant and the animal kingdom live. Be considerate towards them and try not to encroach into their natural habitats.
5. Be aware of activities like mining and quarrying which are destroying our natural landscape and doing irrevocable damage to our planet.

The Good Citizen in Me

Responsibilities of a good citizen

- Follow rules and laws
- Respect the rights of others
- Respect the property of others
- Be honest and trustworthy
- Be compassionate
- Volunteer to help in community activity
- Keep yourself informed about the world around you
- Help to protect the environment

Let this be your 'Good Citizen' Journal.

Whenever you feel that you have done something that proves that you are a good citizen, make an entry in this journal. You can paste pictures, photographs or illustrate to make your journal more interesting. Be honest with your entries and show your good side for the world to see.

_____
_____
_____
_____
_____
_____
_____
_____
_____
_____
_____
_____